FRANKLIN PARK PUBLIC LIBRARY
FRANKLIN PARK, ILL.

BIOGRAPHY FROM
ANCIENT CIVILIZATIONS
LEGENDS, FOLKLORE, AND STORIES OF ANCIENT WORLDS

The Life and Times of

HIPPOCRATES

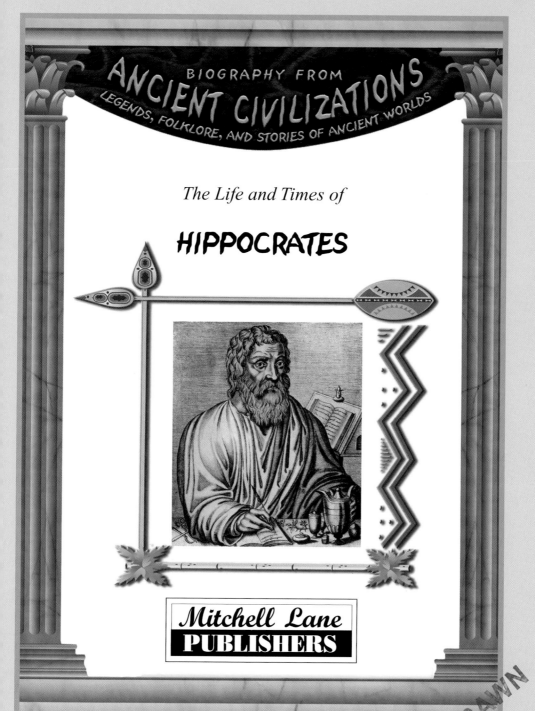

Mitchell Lane
PUBLISHERS

P.O. Box 196
Hockessin, Delaware 19707

BIOGRAPHY FROM ANCIENT CIVILIZATIONS
LEGENDS, FOLKLORE, AND STORIES OF ANCIENT WORLDS

Titles in the Series

The Life and Times of:

BIOGRAPHY FROM
ANCIENT CIVILIZATIONS
LEGENDS, FOLKLORE, AND STORIES OF ANCIENT WORLDS

The Life and Times of

HIPPOCRATES

Jim Whiting

Copyright © 2007 by Mitchell Lane Publishers, Inc. All rights reserved. No part of this book may be reproduced without written permission from the publisher. Printed and bound in the United States of America.

Printing   1   2   3   4   5   6   7   8   9

Library of Congress Cataloging-in-Publication Data

Whiting, Jim, 1943–
     The life and times of Hippocrates/by Jim Whiting.
          p. cm.—(Biography from ancient civilizations)
     Includes bibliographical references and index.
     ISBN 1-58415-512-4 (library bound: alk. paper)
1. Hippocrates—Juvenile literature. 2. Medicine, Greek and Roman. 3. Physicians—
Biography. I. Title. II. Series.
R126.H8W45 2006
610.92—dc22   2005036807
ISBN-10: 1-58415-512-4   ISBN-13: 978-1-58415-512-6

ABOUT THE AUTHOR: Jim Whiting has been a remarkably versatile and accomplished journalist, writer, editor, and photographer for more than 30 years. A voracious reader since early childhood, Mr. Whiting has written and edited about 200 nonfiction children's books. His subjects range from authors to zoologists and include contemporary pop icons and classical musicians, saints and scientists, emperors and explorers. Representative titles include *The Life and Times of Franz Liszt*, *The Life and Times of Julius Caesar*, *Charles Schulz*, and *Juan Ponce de Leon*.

      Other career highlights are a lengthy stint publishing *Northwest Runner*, the first piece of original fiction to appear in *Runners World* magazine, hundreds of descriptions and venue photographs for America Online, e-commerce product writing, sports editor for the *Bainbridge Island Review*, light verse in a number of magazines, and acting as the official photographer for the Antarctica Marathon

      He lives in Washington state with his wife and two teenage sons.

PHOTO CREDITS: Cover, pp. 1, 3, 6—Getty Images; pp. 8, 11—Corbis; p. 16—Getty Images; p. 19—Corbis; p. 24—Andrea Pickens; pp. 32, 38—Corbis

PUBLISHER'S NOTE: This story is based on the author's extensive research, which he believes to be accurate. Documentation of such research is contained on page 46.
The internet sites referenced herein were active as of the publication date. Due to the fleeting nature of some web sites, we cannot guarantee they will all be active when you are reading this book.
      To reflect current usage, we have chosen to use the secular era designations BCE ("before the common era") and CE ("of the common era") instead of the traditional designations BC ("before Christ") and AD (*anno Domini*, "in the year of the Lord").

The Life and Times of

HIPPOCRATES

*For Your Information

No one knows what Hippocrates actually looked like. This portrait was made many centuries after his death. The artist emphasized Hippocrates' books and medicine. These illustrate the importance Hippocrates placed on understanding the natural causes of illness.

CHAPTER
ONE

TIME-TESTED MEDICAL TREATMENTS

On September 23, 2005, President George W. Bush presented Tibor "Ted" Rubin with the Congressional Medal of Honor. It is the highest military award in the United States. Normally it is awarded for extraordinary heroism in battle. Rubin had indeed been a battlefield hero during the Korean War. His medal also honored him for extraordinary heroism in captivity. His fellow prisoners-of-war (POWs) estimated that he saved scores of American lives. He would sneak out of the prison camp to steal desperately needed food. It was very risky. He would have been shot or tortured if he had been caught.

Food wasn't his only contribution. Many of his fellow POWs suffered from battlefield wounds to their arms and legs. Often the wounds became infected. Gangrene would set it in. This dangerous condition involves the death of tissue surrounding the wound. If it isn't treated quickly, it can become so widespread that there are only two alternatives. One is amputating the limb. The other is death.

Rubin saw many of his comrades fall victim to gangrene. He called on his unique "medical training." In 1944, when he was

President George W. Bush (right) congratulates Tibor "Ted" Rubin. President Bush awarded Rubin the Congressional Medal of Honor for his heroism during the Korean War.

just thirteen, Rubin, a Hungarian Jew, had been taken to the World War II German concentration camp at Mauthausen, Austria. The camp was located near a granite quarry. Rubin and the other prisoners there had one primary task: to dig up the granite. The rock would be used to expand the prison and to decorate German homes.

Granite is very hard and heavy. It is normally quarried by blasting powder, heavy air-powered drills, and power saws. Mauthausen adopted a policy called *Primitivbauweise*, or "primitive construction." Prisoners were given only basic hand tools, or sometimes no tools at all. They had to work with their bare hands. Their workday lasted at least twelve hours, and their hands would become raw and bleed. They were fed very little food. They wore only lightweight clothing, even though Austrian winters can be very cold. The Nazis imposed these harsh conditions in order to cause "extermination by work." They largely succeeded: Most of the prisoners perished before the camp was liberated by U.S. troops in May 1945.

Somehow Rubin survived. His parents and his two sisters didn't. Rubin was very grateful to the American soldiers who freed him. He vowed he would join the U.S. Army as soon as he was old enough.

He arrived in the United States soon after his liberation and lived up to his word. He enlisted in the army, even though he wasn't officially a U.S. citizen. In 1950, when North Korea invaded South Korea, thousands of American troops were sent to help the South Koreans. Rubin was one of them. His commanding officer told him he didn't have to go, since he wasn't a citizen yet. Rubin went anyway.

In November 1950, he was wounded and captured. He and his fellow POWs were sent to a prison camp they quickly named "Death Valley." Again Rubin had to endure a horrible captivity. There was little food. Medical care was almost nonexistent. The men faced bitter winters wearing summer-weight clothing. Dozens of men died every day. Rubin didn't.

As he watched his friends suffer, Rubin revived a medical skill that he had learned at Mauthausen. Gangrene had been common there. Rubin and the other inmates realized that maggots—the larvae of houseflies—helped to cure gangrene.

The little creatures secrete a chemical that breaks down the infected tissue into a sort of soup. Then the hungry larvae slurp it up. When they remove the diseased tissue, recovery soon follows.

The chemical leaves healthy tissue alone. It also contains a sort of antibiotic, which helps the healing process by fighting germs.

Rotting meat is one good source of larvae. There was hardly any meat for the POWs. The same thing had been true at Mauthausen. There is, however, another source of nourishment for the larvae: human excrement.

At Mauthausen, Rubin had become accustomed to descending into the latrines to gather maggots. He did the same thing in his POW camp. Each time, he scooped up handfuls of fecal matter and picked out the squirming white legless larvae. He placed them on the wounds of his friends. Rubin's efforts paid off. His "treatment" prevented scores of American soldiers from losing their limbs or their lives.

We may think of "maggot therapy" as a disgusting throwback to more primitive times; after all, the treatment is more than three thousand years old. It is difficult to conceive of people using it unless they are in the same desperate conditions that Rubin faced. Yet maggot therapy is becoming increasingly popular in mainstream medicine. It has been used to treat thousands of patients in recent years. Scores of practitioners who do maggot therapy are listed in a nationwide database. In 2004, the U.S. Food and Drug Administration (FDA), which protects the public health, approved the use of maggots for treating several types of injuries.

Maggots have a number of advantages over more conventional treatments. They are cheap. They are natural. Most important, they can be effective in treating conditions when modern drugs fail.

Maggots have been recognized as nature's little healers. Hundreds at a time are placed on certain types of wounds. Sometimes using maggots is a more effective cure than more common forms of medical treatment.

Maggots aren't the only creepy-crawlies making a comeback in modern medicine. Leeches are too. They are bloodsucking, wormlike creatures several inches long that live in water. They feed by attaching themselves to an animal. They suck the animal's blood until they are full. Then they fall off.

The FDA okayed the medicinal use of leeches at about the same time it gave the nod of approval to maggots. The ruling marked the first time that the organization had approved the use of live animals as "medical devices." If the leeches could talk, they might say, "It's about time!" Their history as medical cures goes back at least as far as that of maggots.

One of their most notable uses came during the fifth century BCE. For hundreds of years, people had regarded illness and disease as punishments that came from the gods. A Greek physician named Hippocrates changed that outlook. He ceased looking for supernatural reasons. He based his treatments on close observation of people suffering from illness and wounds.

As a result of his observations, he formed a theory involving the four humors. He believed that the human body contained four fluids, or humors. These were blood, phlegm, black bile, and yellow bile. Each humor was associated with a particular organ and emotion. Blood came from the heart and helped make people cheerful. Phlegm was centered in the brain and aided in calmness. The spleen was the home of black bile, which could lead to depression and a gloomy outlook. Yellow bile, from the liver, led to anger, a hot temper, and courage.

If the four humors were in balance with each other, a person would be in good health. Problems arose when one or more of the humors began to increase or decrease. Then the person would be out of balance. The problem was especially acute in the case of an increase. Somehow the body had to expel the excess, which could occur naturally with vomiting, sweating, or excreting.

It could also occur artificially. A physician would "bleed" a patient by opening a blood vessel and allowing a certain amount of blood to escape. In theory, this bloodletting would restore the balance of the humors and lead to recovery.

Opening blood vessels with a knife was one option. Hippocrates must have observed that the procedure was messy. Blood would often spurt rather than flow. Another problem was that human blood contains a coagulant. This is a built-in safety measure that causes blood to clot, preventing excess blood loss. If the blood clotted before enough had escaped, the physician would have to make another opening. A third problem was that cutting into the skin could lead to a dangerous infection.

Leeches solved all three problems. The little creatures have suction cups at both ends. The rear one helps it move about and hold it in position when it is ready to eat. The front one has three sharp jaws that give a Y-shaped bite. When the leech chomps down and begins to suck its victim's blood, several chemicals in the creature's saliva go to work.

One chemical contains an anesthetic. The victim doesn't feel any pain. Often he or she isn't even aware of the presence of the leech. A second enlarges the blood vessels in the area of the bite. A third fights the blood's tendency to clot when the skin is broken and bleeding begins. Still another helps to prevent swelling. Like maggots, leeches also produce an antibiotic that fights infection. And there is no mess. All the blood goes straight into the hungry leech.

Hippocrates wasn't the only doctor to use leeches in ancient times, but his theory of humors was the first "scientific" explanation to justify the bleeding of patients. Today we know that Hippocrates' theory wasn't correct, but his influence was so strong that people believed in "humors" for more than 2,000 years.

There was another carryover. In England during the Middle Ages, leech therapy was very common. The words *doctor* and *leech* were virtually identical. In fact, the word *leech* comes from an older word that means "to heal."

Leeches are no longer used to bleed people, but doctors have discovered that the little creatures can have a place in operating rooms and recovery areas. They help to keep blood flowing. They drain off excess blood, which helps promote faster healing. They also prevent blood clotting in areas where it can cause extensive tissue damage.

In fact, medical researchers are trying to construct an artificial leech. Real leeches drop off when they are full. An artificial leech would remain in place as long as it is needed.

Hippocrates may also have had experience with maggots. Scholars believe that he suffered from occasional leg ulcers. If so, he might well have used maggots for his own treatment.

Hippocrates has been credited with introducing another type of animal-based treatment: bee-sting therapy. In the therapy's original version, patients allowed themselves to be stung by up to several dozen bees. They believed the stings dramatically increased blood circulation. The improved circulation helped cleanse the body of impurities that could otherwise cause infection. It was also regarded as a way of treating arthritis and other joint-related problems.

Bee-sting therapy is also undergoing a revival and is especially popular in China. "In recent years, we use bees to treat rheumatism, scleroderma and bedsores, and it proves to be quite effective," Han Qiaoju, chief doctor of a bee therapy center in Hebei Province, north China, said in 2001.[1]

Technological advances have spared patients the worst part of the treatment: the stinging itself. Now the venom can be injected directly into the affected area.

These revivals show that Hippocrates isn't just a figure from the distant past. For some sufferers, his groundbreaking medical work may still be just what the doctor ordered.

Other Ancient Animal-Based Therapies

Ancient physicians used other creatures in their work besides maggots, leeches, and bees.

When ancient Indian doctors performed intestinal surgery, they stitched the patient's incision back together. Using needles left tiny holes, and bacteria-laden fluids would leak through them. The fluids could cause serious or even fatal infections.

Ants provided the solution. The physicians would hold an ant next to one end of the incision. The ant's jaws would clamp down, bringing the two edges together. The healers continued putting ant after ant next to each other in a tightly packed row until they reached the other end. Then they'd cut off the ants' bodies. Even in death, the jaws remained locked. The patient's body would eventually turn the ants' heads into mush and absorb them. A similar procedure is still used in some parts of the world.

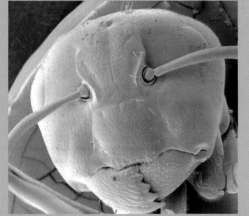

A close-up photo of an ant

The Egyptians used dead mice as a "cure" for toothaches. The "therapy" often consisted of inserting a dead rodent into the sufferer's mouth. They also ground up the little creatures to make medicines. This practice persisted in several cultures well into the twentieth century.

The Egyptians also developed a "cure" for baldness. They concocted a paste from the fats of different animals: cats, crocodiles, snakes, hippos. The physician would smear the paste on the person's head.

Animal fats had a more practical purpose in Egypt. Physicians would lather them next to wounds before applying bandages. That way the bandages wouldn't stick to the skin and cause pain when they were pulled off.

The Romans developed a form of electric shock therapy. They captured electric eels or torpedo fish. The creatures were immersed in large tanks of salt water. Patients were put into the same tanks. The fish gave them repeated high-voltage jolts of electricity. Scholars believe the technique was used to treat joint and muscle pain, and even paralysis. A simpler form of the procedure was used to treat headaches. The animals were placed directly on the head of the patient.

This portrait of the Greek epic poet Homer was painted by Rembrandt van Rijn in 1663. Scholars believe that Homer wrote his long poems "The Iliad" and "The Odyssey" about 800 BCE. In turn, the Trojan War—the subject of the two poems—may have taken place four centuries earlier.

CHAPTER
TWO

EARLY GREEK MEDICINE

Around 1960, archaeologists working in Iraq made an exciting discovery. They turned up a burial ground containing Neanderthal skeletons. Neanderthals were primitive human beings that lived probably about 30,000 to 230,000 years ago.

One of the skeletons was especially interesting. It was a man, about forty years old. He was badly crippled. One arm was withered. Arthritis had twisted his body into a grotesque shape. His teeth were extremely worn. The archaeologists believed his tribe didn't abandon him. Instead, they took care of him. Perhaps his teeth were so worn because he chewed on animal skins to soften them for clothing. It may have been his way of contributing to the tribe.

"Even more remarkable is the strong likelihood that one of his tribe had actually performed surgery on him, for the skeleton's right arm is missing from just above the elbow," write researchers Peter James and Nick Thorpe. "The end of the arm bone has a rounded surface, suggesting it may have healed up after the operation."[1]

If the amputation actually took place, it must have been among the first human medical procedures. It would have been incredibly painful. The cutting tools available then were made of sharpened stones. It would have taken a long time to cut through flesh and bone with those. The person who performed the amputation wouldn't have had any special training.

Other scholars dispute the idea that an amputation took place. They suggest that the arm may have become deformed as the result of an accident. But one thing is plain: Human beings have always suffered from a variety of medical problems. Some were natural, such as illnesses, diseases, and animal attacks. Others, such as battle wounds, were caused by humans. As the world's population increased, so did the desire to help these victims.

About 4,500 years ago, records were kept of people who had special training in medicine. The records are from ancient Sumer and Egypt.

Nevertheless, recovery even after treatment by trained medical personnel was often hit-or-miss. The inner workings of the human body were still largely a mystery. To the doctors as well as their patients, survival often appeared to be something beyond their control. It seemed to be at the whim of the gods.

This belief was especially common among the Greeks. Their important stories, such as Homer's *Iliad* and *Odyssey*, are filled with accounts of gods becoming involved in human health crises. Hera, the wife of the chief god Zeus, helps in childbirth. Apollo sends plagues when he is upset with the way people behave. He stops these plagues when their behavior improves. Apollo sent his infant son, Asclepius, to live with a centaur named Chiron. Chiron, who had invented medicine, taught the child everything he knew.

A Roman statue of the Greek god Apollo. In addition to his connection with the practice of medicine, Apollo had many other attributes. He was considered the god of light, noted for the practice of archery, and connected with the act of thinking clearly.

There could be a germ of historical fact in this story. Asclepius may have been based on an actual person. Over time, his special healing talents made him seem almost godlike, so he became worshiped as a god. Asclepius had at least two daughters. One was Hygeia, which means "health." Our word *hygiene* comes from her name. The other daughter was Panacea. Today, *panacea* means "cure-all."

Chiron also taught the hero Achilles. Achilles was one of the central Greek warriors to fight in the Trojan War. Achilles' healing skills were nearly as renowned as his ability with sword and spear.

At one point in *The Iliad*, Homer's account of the Trojan War, a Greek warrior named Eurypylus has been wounded in the thigh by an arrow. He encounters Patroclus, Achilles' best friend. Patroclus has acquired his friend's medical skills. Eurypylus says to Patroclus,

> Save me at least. Take me back to my black ship,
> Cut this shaft from my thigh. And the dark blood—
> wash it out of the wound with clear warm water.
> And spread the soothing, healing salves across it,
> the powerful drugs they say you learned from Achilles
> And Chiron the most humane of Centaurs taught your friend.[2]

Patroclus cuts out the arrow with a knife, washes the wound with cold water. Then

> He crushed a bitter root
> and covered over the gash to kill his comrade's pain,
> a cure that fought off every kind of pain . . .
> and the wound dried and the flowing blood stopped.[3]

Eurypylus was one of the lucky ones. He apparently lived to fight another day. Most other wounded Greek warriors weren't as fortunate. Many of the treatments Homer describes start with healthy soldiers sucking the wound. Then they apply herbs to the affected area. This "treatment" didn't help much. Scholars have counted about 150 instances of battle wounds in *The Iliad*. The mortality rate was about 70 percent.

Homer probably wrote during the eighth century BCE. Sometimes a god was responsible for the wounds he describes. Sometimes it was another human being. In either case, the device used to inflict the wound was visible: a sword, a spear, a heavy club, an arrow.

Illnesses and accidents were something else. They seemed to strike at random. Often they were regarded as the will of the gods. People frequently viewed themselves as helpless victims. For defense, they turned to prayer. Sanctuaries dedicated to Asclepius, the god of healing, began to sprout up. Soon there were more than a hundred of these Asclepia (uh-SKLEE-pee-uh).

The most famous was at Epidaurus, which in modern times has become a popular tourist site. In it was a theater that held up to 16,000 people. Even today, its acoustics are excellent. Visitors stand in the center of the stage and speak in low voices. Their friends in the top rows can easily hear them.

In ancient times, the theater would have been secondary. The main attraction was the temple to Asclepius.

The temples varied, but each included a large statue of the god. In some, he carries a staff with a single snake coiled around it. In others, two snakes coil around each other. Snakes were sacred to the Greeks. Some researchers believe the Greeks had discovered that small doses of snake venom could cure various illnesses.

The "patients" couldn't be too ill. It would have shown disrespect to Asclepius to die in his holy precinct. Nor was there an emergency room. Patients had to wait their turn, staying at inns nearby.

While there, they were put on strict diets. They often bathed in cold water. Their surroundings were serene and peaceful. Perhaps most beneficial of all, they knew that they wouldn't be subjected to the primitive medical treatments of the day. No one would dig into them. Each day they eagerly read about the cures that had occurred the previous day.

After waiting for several days, sick people were finally taken inside the temple. They would offer a libation (a liquid sacrifice, such as blood or wine, to the gods) and a donation and put on white clothing. Upbeat priests discussed the likelihood of a cure. That night, the sufferers would go to sleep in beds inside the temple. They were blindfolded. Asclepius, one of his daughters, or a sacred snake or dog would appear in a dream. In the morning, the priest would awaken them. In theory, the sick would be cured.

One of the fortunate patients was a man named Gorgias. A marker at Epidaurus records his happy outcome: "In a battle he had been wounded by an arrow in the lung and for a year and a half he had suppurated so badly that he filled sixty-seven basins with pus. While sleeping in the temple he saw a vision. It seemed to him the god extracted the arrowhead from his lung. When day came, he walked out well, holding the arrowhead in his hands."[4]

It is likely that at least some of the cures came from the power of suggestion. In modern times, supposedly terminally ill people have recovered because of their positive mental outlook. This would have been just as plausible twenty-five centuries ago.

Many Greeks believed completely in the power and effectiveness of the Asclepia. Others were more skeptical. There were stories of patients peeking out from under their blindfolds. They saw servants steal their possessions. Sometimes what they witnessed was more reprehensible. One patient left a vivid description: "Glancing upwards, I behold the priest whipping the cheese-cakes and the figs from off the holy table; thence he coasted round to every altar, spying what was left. And everything he found he consecrated into a sort of sack."[5]

The Greeks needed something better. They got it.

The Trojan War

The story of the Trojan War begins with a competition among three ancient goddesses. Athena, Hera, and Aphrodite each believes she is more beautiful than the other two. They choose Paris, a Trojan prince, to be the judge.

Each offers him a bribe. He chooses Aphrodite's—the love of Helen, the most beautiful woman in the world. Helen is already married, though, to Menelaus, an important Greek king.

When Paris takes Helen home with him, Menelaus is furious. He calls on the other kings of Greece to come to his aid, and a huge fleet sails to Troy. The most famous Greek soldier is Achilles. According to legend, his mother dipped him in the River Styx to protect him from death. She gripped him by the heel, so the water didn't touch him there. His heel was his one vulnerable spot. Late in the war, an arrow strikes him in the heel, and he dies.

Aphrodite

The war lasts for ten years. The Greeks can't get inside the city's defensive walls. Finally they pretend to sail away. They leave behind a huge wooden horse that contains a small group of Greeks. The Trojans haul it inside, believing it to be a gift from Athena. When everyone in the city is asleep, the Greeks climb down and open the city gates. Meanwhile, under cover of darkness, the Greek ships have sailed back. Thousands of warriors pour into the city. They slaughter many Trojans and enslave the rest.

The story was well documented in the ancient world. Homer's epic poems *The Iliad* and *The Odyssey* detail the war and its aftermath. Later, people doubted the truth of the stories. They didn't believe that Troy even existed. In the late nineteenth century, Heinrich Schliemann discovered the ruins of Troy. Today, many scholars believe that there had been a war between the Greeks and the Trojans. It may have been waged around 1200 BCE. However, they don't feel that Helen had anything to do with it. The most likely cause was an economic or territorial dispute.

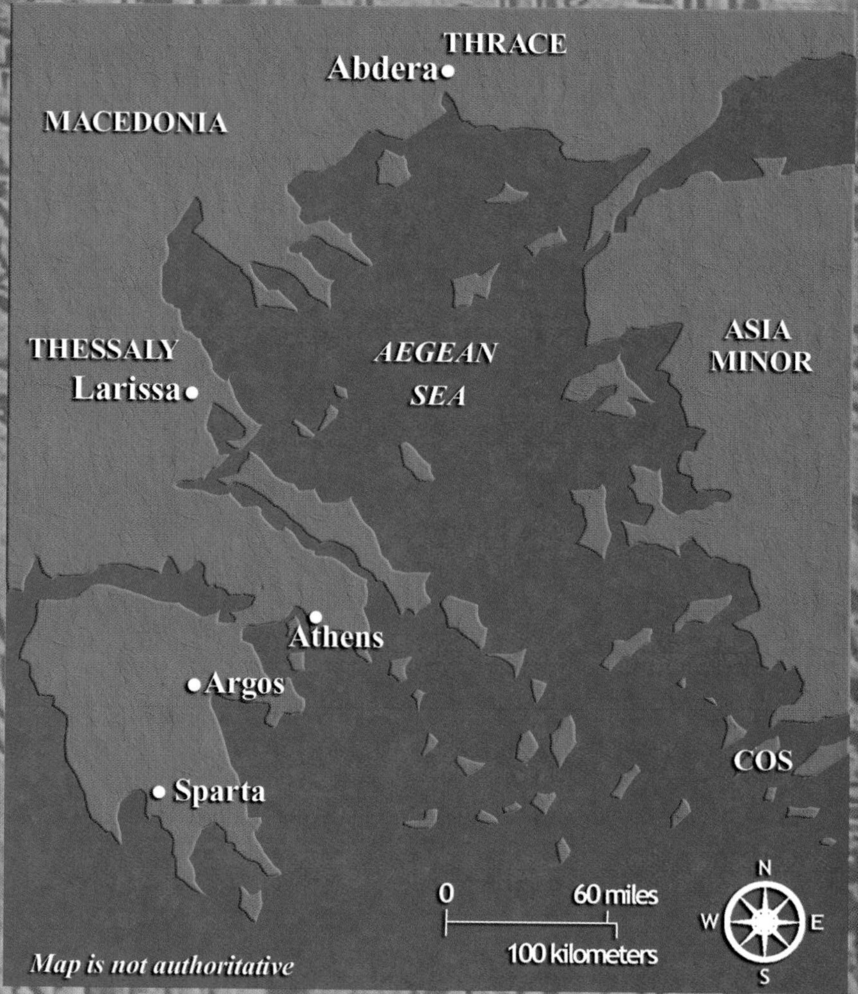

THRACE

Abdera•

MACEDONIA

THESSALY

Larissa•

AEGEAN
SEA

ASIA
MINOR

Athens○

•Argos

•Sparta

COS

0   60 miles

100 kilometers

N
W   E
S

Map is not authoritative

This map illustrates many places associated with Hippocrates' travels. It's possible that he didn't actually visit all of them. The ones with the highest degree of certainty are Cos (where he was born and grew up) and Larissa (the site of his death).

CHAPTER
THREE

A LEGENDARY LIFE

Very little is known about the life of Hippocrates. Because the respected Greek philosophers Plato and Aristotle both mention him in their works, scholars are confident that he did exist. They are equally confident that he was an outstanding physician who put medicine on a scientific footing.

No one knows why Hippocrates decided to make such a dramatic break with the past. Part of the reason is likely that he was in the right place at the right time.

The Greeks had been developing new ways of thinking for decades before his birth. Near the end of the sixth century BCE, they invented a new form of government: democracy. Prior to that, countries were under the control of kings or groups of aristocrats.

The Greeks were also trying to understand the world around them. For centuries, they had believed that whatever happened to them was the will of the gods. Now they were taking a much closer look at the natural causes of events.

It was an ideal environment for a man such as Hippocrates.

Much of what we know about Hippocrates' life comes from a man named Soranus of Cos, who wrote about 500 years afterward. Soranus begins with what may be a factual note. He says that Hippocrates was born on the Greek island of Cos (a few miles off the southwestern coast of modern-day Turkey) in 460 BCE. His father was Herakleides. His mother was named Phenarete.

Hippocrates' father was a doctor. So was his father before him. And so it went, back and back, to Asclepius. Soranus was saying that Hippocrates was a direct descendent of the god of healing.

Soranus gives no details of Hippocrates' childhood. It's likely from a young age he knew he would be a physician. Soranus emphasizes that Hippocrates received not just medical training but also a general education. He was exposed to some of the era's most important thinkers. These thinkers were seeking natural rather than supernatural explanations for the world around them.

At some point—perhaps when he was in his early twenties—Hippocrates left Cos. There are several explanations for his departure. His parents had died, and he apparently had no family ties to bind him to his home. With the interest in the natural world that became his trademark, he may well have wanted to see how people in other areas practiced medicine. He traveled widely through the ancient Greek world. According to one story, he fled the island one step ahead of the law. He burned down a rival medical school that was located nearby and had to leave to avoid being punished. Yet another explanation is that in a dream he was ordered to go to the Greek region of Thessaly. The Greeks took dreams very seriously.

Once Hippocrates was "on the road," Soranus doesn't provide any chronology. He records several incidents, but there is no indication as to when they happened or even if they happened in the order in which he wrote them down.

One of Hippocrates' patients was Perdiccas, the king of Macedonia. He was very ill. He wanted Hippocrates to tell him whether he was going to die. Hippocrates performed an extensive physical examination. He realized that Perdiccas' problems were primarily mental. He was in love. Unfortunately, he was in love with the same woman whom his deceased father had loved. As we might say today, Perdiccas was conflicted. Hippocrates managed to cure him.

On another occasion, he was summoned by the city-state of Abdera in Thrace, one of Greece's northernmost regions. A famous philosopher named Democritus lived there. His fellow citizens believed he was insane, and they wanted Hippocrates to heal him. Hippocrates talked with Democritus. He concluded that he wasn't insane. He was simply different from the other people of Abdera.

His skills apparently extended to diplomacy. Athens threatened his home island of Cos with invasion. Hippocrates appealed to the Thessalians to help. They must have agreed. The invasion was called off.

Athens bore him no grudge. Besides the citizens in Thessaly, Cos, and Argos (another city-state), the Athenians also showered him with honors. They granted him Athenian citizenship—something hardly ever done for those who hadn't been born in the polis—and allowed him and his descendents to eat free anytime they were in the city.

Hippocrates was also patriotic. Soranus mentions several non-Greek kingdoms that asked him to assist them. On one occasion, a kingdom north of Greece requested his help with a plague that was sweeping the country. He determined that the same disease would soon descend on Greece. His fellow Greeks deserved his assistance more, he decided. He didn't make the trip.

The Persians, the longtime enemies of the Greeks, also wanted him to help. They offered him a great deal of money. Hippocrates turned them down. "This was due to his dignity, indifference to money, and love of home,"[1] Soranus comments.

Soranus adds one more quality. Hippocrates didn't keep his knowledge to himself. He freely and happily passed it along.

According to Soranus, Hippocrates died in the city of Larissa, Thessaly. The traditional date is 377. That would have made him 83. Other sources provide a range of dates from 380 to 351. He left behind two sons, Thessalos and Dracon, and many students. Both of his sons followed him into the medical profession.

Soranus adds that Hippocrates' burial site endured for several centuries. In view of his pioneering work with bees, it is significant that bees swarmed into his tomb. They produced honey that mothers used to help their babies recover from thrush, a fungal disease common among children.

That is about all. The incidents that Soranus chooses to mention all took place when Hippocrates was famous. He doesn't include any details about why he was able to reach this level of fame. This omission is troubling to many scholars. They believe that Hippocrates was almost a household word in the Greek-speaking world. They would like to know why.

As classics professor Edwin Burton Levine sarcastically notes of Soranus, "The truth was simply ignored in favor of all sorts of nonsense calculated to dazzle the innocent and impress the gullible. Where we should be pleased . . . to have the facts of his ancestry, birth (including the all-important dates of birth and death), and a scheme at least of his youthful training and subsequent professional activity through the years of his maturity, the surviving biographical notes tell us only the wonderful, the miraculous, the improbable, or the impossible."[2]

There may be one more detail. Soranus doesn't mention it but other ancient writers do. At that time there was no such thing as the "country" of Greece. Rather, it was a collection of dozens of tiny city-states. Also known as polises, these city-states consisted of a central city or town and the surrounding countryside. They were linked by a common alphabet and language, religion (nearly all worshiped the same major gods, though most also had a few that were unique), and the Olympic Games.

In spite of their common elements, most of the polises didn't get along with one another. Their disagreements came to a head in 431 with the outbreak of the Peloponnesian War. The major rivals were Sparta and Athens. Many of the other poleis became involved, fighting on one side or the other. It was a mini–world war.

Soon afterward, a devastating plague struck Athens and carried off a significant portion of the population. Noted ancient historian Thucydides described the symptoms: It began with headaches, painful red eyes, bleeding from the mouth, sneezing, hoarseness, and coughing. Next came stomachaches and severe vomiting. The skin broke out with open sores. Then the body temperature rose so high that people couldn't bear to wear anything.

The fever killed many. The ones who lived on faced uncontrolled diarrhea, painful stomach ulcers, and sometimes blindness. A number of them soon perished.

The disease was very contagious. Those who tried to help the victims often succumbed themselves. These included many of the city's physicians. Bodies lay unburied. People were afraid to touch them. The stench was horrible.[3]

According to some sources, Hippocrates cured the disease, or at least helped to bring the plague under control. If so, it would have been relatively close to the beginning of his career. It would certainly help to account for his subsequent fame. Anyone who could go one-on-one with a horrible disease and win would have become an instant celebrity.

While he doesn't specifically identify Hippocrates with the plague, a second-century CE Roman writer named Aulus Gellius provides additional evidence for Hippocrates' fame: "Then the great Peloponnesian War began in Greece, which Thucydides has handed down to memory. . . . During that period Sophocles, and later Euripides, were famous and renowned as tragic poets, Hippocrates as a physician, and as a philosopher, Democritus; Socrates the Athenian was younger than these, but was in part their contemporary."[4]

On a personal level, Hippocrates seems to have been somewhat modest. He wasn't the type of person who would toot his own horn. Yet we do know a great deal about his methods. Soranus may have left behind only a few hundred words. Hippocrates left behind many thousands.

Greek Words in Medicine

People often say, "It's Greek to me." The phrase means they don't understand what someone is talking about.

To modern-day physicians, however, "It's Greek to me" has an entirely different meaning. Many words they use on a regular basis come directly from Greek. This is another example of the influence of Hippocrates.

Medicine has moved beyond Hippocrates' theory of the four humors, yet several words from the theory remain in common use. A person who is *melancholy* (from the Greek words for "black bile") is depressed. Someone *sanguine* (from "blood") is hopeful. *Cholera* is a disease that involves severe diarrhea and can be fatal. The word comes from *choler* ("yellow bile") and describes an extreme method of getting rid of excess yellow bile. A *phlegmatic* person is slow-moving or calm.

Sometimes we say that a person is in an *ill humor,* meaning "in a bad mood." Because courage was associated with yellow bile, we call a coward *yellow*—meaning the person lacks yellow bile.

Many diseases have Greek names. *Pneumonia* is a serious lung condition (from *pneumon,* "lung"). *Asthma* refers to breathing difficulties (the root means "I pant"). *Bronchitis,* from the Greek word for "windpipe," is yet another respiratory problem. *Arthritis* ("joint disease") affects joints such as knees.

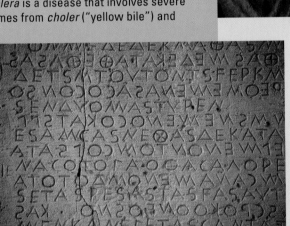

Ancient Greek writing

Many medical specialties also have Greek names. A *cardiologist* is a heart surgeon. A *gynecologist* treats women. An *ophthalmologist* takes care of eyes. A *podiatrist* is a foot specialist. A *pediatrician* sees children. All five roots mean exactly the same in Greek.

Some words combine several Greek roots. For example, an *electrocardiogram* means literally "using electricity to write about the heart." The test uses wires fastened to a patient's chest to check the functioning of his or her heart.

In Hippocrates' time, the word *epidemic* referred to the journeys of a physician to visit various groups of people. It literally means "among people." Nowadays, an epidemic is a different kind of "journey." It is the journey of a fast-moving disease that infects a large number of people.

One of the most widely reported episodes of the healer's life was when Hippocrates (seated on the left) resisted a request to aid the king of Persia. The king reportedly offered him a great deal of money, but Hippocrates turned him down. He felt it was more important to take care of his fellow Greeks.

CHAPTER
FOUR

THE HIPPOCRATIC COLLECTION

We know a lot about ancient Greek medicine because of the *Hippocratic Collection*. It consists of about seventy manuscripts that deal with various medical conditions. Hippocrates may have written all of them—or none of them.

Soranus was aware of this fact. "Much disagreement has arisen about his works, and a variety of conjectures has been made," he wrote. "Therefore, it is not easy to give one's opinion about them because many factors cloud one's judgement."[1]

It seems probable that Hippocrates wrote at least some of the manuscripts. His followers may have written the remainder over a period of several decades. This time frame would account for the fact that the writings in some parts of the *Collection* appear to contradict other parts.

The most famous part of the *Hippocratic Collection* is the Hippocratic Oath. It consists of ethical principles that new physicians swore to uphold.

Another famous part of the *Collection* deals with epilepsy, a condition that was apparently much more common in ancient times than it is today. As Hippocrates describes the symptoms, "the patient becomes speechless and chokes; froth flows from the mouth; he gnashes his teeth and twists his hands; the eyes roll and intelligence fails him and in some cases excrement is discharged."[2]

These symptoms—which came on suddenly and without warning—were very spectacular to early onlookers. They believed that the disease came directly from the gods. They called it "the sacred disease."

Nonsense, said Hippocrates (or one of his followers). Only "witch-doctors, faith-healers, quacks and charlatans" believe in attacks from the gods, and prescribe "purifications, incantations, prohibition of baths, lying on goat-skins and eating goats' flesh."[3]

The disease has nothing to do with the gods, the writer continues. It is caused by a disturbance in the brain. Phlegm— one of the four humors—builds up in the brain. It obstructs the blood vessels in the skull. The condition is especially likely to occur during certain weather conditions, such as the change of seasons. At these times, sufferers need to take special precautions. The writer concludes, "Whoever is acquainted with such a change in man and can render a man humid and dry, hot and cold by regimen can also cure this disease—without minding purifications, spells, and all other illiberal practices of a like kind."[4]

The rest of the *Collection* takes similar positions. All diseases can be explained on the basis of the natural world. No supernatural explanations are necessary.

Hippocrates didn't try to deny the effectiveness of the Asclepia. He recognized that they were effective for some people. There was even a famous one on his home island of Cos.

One of the things that especially distinguished Hippocrates and his followers was their insistence on keeping detailed descriptions of the actual procedures they employed. Some were relatively mild: fasting, hot baths, the use of warm sponges, even inserting peeled onions into the nostrils to help overcome the side effects of excessive drinking of alcoholic beverages.

A few sound especially painful. For example, the cure for hemorrhoids was to apply a red-hot iron to the patient's anus.

The *Collection* also documents individual case studies.

"The maiden daughter of Euryanix was seized with fever," begins one. "Throughout the illness she suffered no thirst and had no inclination for food. . . . She had a rigor; grew slightly hot, sweated. Afterwards the extremities always cold. About the tenth day, after the sweating that occurred, she grew delirious. . . . They said the trouble was due to eating grapes. . . . The bowels were disturbed, with bilious, uncompounded, scanty, thin, irritating stools, which frequently made her get up. She died the seventh day from the second attack of delirium."[5]

"Another man who dined when hot and drank too much vomited everything during the night, he had acute fever and pain in the [stomach] with inflammation, though there was a feeling of softness underneath the belly wall from the inner part," says another. "He had an uncomfortable night; the urine at first was thick and red, it did not settle on standing; the tongue was dry and there was great thirst. The fourth day there was acute fever with pain all over. On the fifth day he passed much smooth oily urine. Death on the eleventh day."[6] It's not clear what disease Hippocrates was describing, though it may have been a serious ulcer.

Not every case study had such a grim outcome. Some are similar to "the daughter of Pausanias, who had the misfortune to eat raw mushrooms; she became nauseated, had pain in the belly. . . . She was given warm honey, after which she vomited and was placed in a warm bath. In the bath she vomited the meal of mushrooms and as she improved she perspired freely."[7]

The *Collection* contains a number of aphorisms. These are short, easy-to-remember phrases. "Life is short, whereas the demands of the art [medical profession] are unending, the crisis is urgent, experiment dangerous, and decision is difficult," reads the very first one. "But the physician must not only do what is necessary, he must also get the patient, the attendants, and the external factors to work together to the same end."[8]

These demands are just as true today. Professor Levine comments that this aphorism points out "the extraordinary pressures which the professional man must contend with in the practice of medicine."[9]

From the *Collection*, a set of operating principles and general principles emerges. The physician carefully observes his patient, taking note of the symptoms. He looks for natural causes, not supernatural ones. He emphasizes prevention of illness. His prescriptions include attention to diet and physical exercise such as walking. The physician's purpose is to assist nature. Hippocrates frequently urged his patients to walk or even run. He viewed nature as his most powerful ally.

Above all, Hippocrates was well aware of the importance of a positive bedside manner: "For some patients, though conscious that their condition is perilous, recover their health simply through their contentment with the goodness of the physician."[10]

History has rewarded Hippocrates for giving his name to this invaluable document. He is known as the Father of Western Medicine.

It would be up to his "children" to improve on what he had done.

The Hippocratic Oath

No one knows whether Hippocrates or one of his followers wrote the Hippocratic Oath. It doesn't really matter—Hippocrates was the important influence on medical science. His ideas were so important, many doctors and other medical professionals still take an updated version of the oath.

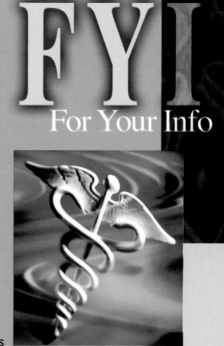

Part of the Hippocratic Oath requires that physicians "do no harm." Reputable doctors still believe in that. They also accept the necessity for doctor-patient confidentiality—another of the elements of the oath.

Two other elements—the refusal to administer deadly drugs or to give an abortion—have become especially controversial in modern times. Some physicians believe in "death with dignity." To end patient suffering, they provide lethal drugs to those who have no chance of surviving a crippling, painful illness. Other doctors believe in giving abortions under certain circumstances. Emotions run very high on both sides of these issues.

The oath is the first code of ethics for any particular profession. It remains the most famous and the most influential. It also had a practical purpose. Ancient Greece was filled with people who claimed mastery of the healing arts. Those who took the oath put themselves on a higher level than their competitors.

In its original version, the oath opens with a prayer to Apollo and the other gods and goddesses associated with healing. No one today who takes the oath swears to these deities. It's likely that Hippocrates included the gods because he never intended to do away with them entirely. He respected them. He just wanted to be sure that people realized that they had some control over their own health.

The oath also had a reward at the end for carrying out its precepts:

Accordingly, if I carry out the provisions of this solemn oath, and if I do not violate any of them, may it be my reward to enjoy life and the practice of my profession, honored always by all men; but if I transgress any provision or falsely swear to this oath, may I suffer the opposite fate.[11]

Galen was the most famous doctor in the Roman Empire. He used Hippocrates' findings and combined them with later research. He was the personal physician to emperor Marcus Aurelius.

CHAPTER
FIVE

AFTER HIPPOCRATES

Alexander the Great was one of Hippocrates' first "children." He was born in 356 BCE, perhaps some twenty years after Hippocrates died. He became king of Macedonia when he was twenty. Before his death in 323, he had conquered nearly two million square miles of territory.

One of Alexander's first conquests was Egypt. In 332 BCE, he founded the city of Alexandria in the Nile Delta region of Egypt. It was ruled by Ptolemy, one of Alexander's generals. Ptolemy founded the final dynasty of Egyptian rulers, or pharaohs. The last member of the dynasty was the famous Cleopatra.

For many years, Alexandria served as the center of Greek culture. It was well known for its library. Many scholars believe that the library contained the *Hippocratic Collection*. Otherwise the manuscripts might have disappeared.

Eventually the center of power in the Mediterranean shifted to Rome. An eminent Roman doctor was Galen. Born in 129 CE, he began his medical career treating wounded gladiators. Well aware of the *Hippocratic Collection*, he expanded Hippocrates'

Alexander the Great studied medicine from Greek philosopher Aristotle. The library in Alexandria, the city Alexander founded in Egypt, most likely housed the Hippocratic Collection.

theory of the four humors. He also published a great deal of his own material. His reputation rivaled that of Hippocrates himself.

Several centuries later, the Roman Empire fell. The rise of Christianity had already destroyed much of the influence of so-called pagan writing. A few scholars managed to save the ancient Greek texts. They fled to the East. There, the rising new religion of Islam welcomed these scholars. For centuries, the Islamic world was the Western world's primary center of knowledge. Muslim doctors incorporated Hippocrates' ideas into their own practice.

A few centuries later, the historical pendulum swung the other way. Knowledge of the ancient world returned to Western Europe. This included the works of Hippocrates.

Nearly two millennia after his death, his writings again were widely regarded as the last word in medical practice. In 1651, a vocal English physician named James Primrose quoted him, saying, "Hippocrates [says] that a physician which like a Philosopher, is God-like."[1] Medical examinations well into the following century included questions about Hippocrates' practices and theories.

It didn't take long for European medical practitioners to follow Hippocrates' own advice. They began conducting their own observations. They quickly discovered that he had not been right in many areas. That led to the explosion in medical knowledge and technology that continues to this day.

Because his conclusions were so often wrong, it may be tempting to say that Hippocrates is no longer useful or relevant. This seems especially true of his prohibition against practicing surgery. For centuries, true physicians regarded surgery as beneath them. They believed that surgeons didn't have the necessary intelligence to become physicians. Even into the Middle Ages, many surgeons were barbers who performed operations as a sideline. Today, of course, surgeons are highly skilled professionals. They have years of specialized training. They routinely perform operations that would have seemed almost godlike to Hippocrates. One of these is brain surgery. In his time, it was a horrible procedure.

In other respects, modern medicine has not been able to improve on Hippocrates. When a patient came to him, Hippocrates conducted a physical examination. On the basis of what he discovered, he made a diagnosis. He concluded what was wrong with the sufferer. He also offered a prognosis, a prediction about the outcome of the patient's condition.

Doctors still do the same two things today. When the examination is complete, they give their diagnosis and prognosis. They may also offer some advice: "Eat well and sensibly, get some exercise, make sure you get a good night's sleep, and call me in the morning."

It's not hard to imagine Hippocrates giving the same instructions.

How Hippocrates Performed Brain Surgery

Many ancient cultures performed a type of brain surgery known as trephining. Hippocrates gave the procedure a scientific foundation. He was especially concerned with blows to the head. Such shocks could lead to a buildup of blood and pus inside the skull. The fluids had to have some way of escaping—otherwise they would press against the brain.

The skull is not a solid mass of bone. It has several natural fissures, or very narrow cracks, but these fissures are not large enough to allow the fluids to escape. If the blow caused a fracture, the resulting crack would provide a large enough opening.

When treating someone with a head injury, Hippocrates shaved the skull at the point of the blow. Then he made an incision in the scalp. An assistant pulled apart the two sides of the incision. Hippocrates smeared a black substance resembling shoe polish on the exposed bone. The next day he scraped off the substance.

If the blow had created cracks, the black would reveal them. The victim undoubtedly breathed a sigh of relief. The fluid had a way of escaping. Apart from the pain—which drugs could help ease—no further action would be taken.

If there was no black—if the blow hadn't caused a fracture—the next step consisted of boring a hole into the skull. There were several types of bone drills. The basic principle was the same with each one. The physician would rotate the drill quickly back and forth with his hands. Eventually he would make a hole in the skull. It must have been unbelievably painful.

People use the same principle as trephining when they want to start a fire but have no matches. The constant rotation causes friction. Friction leads to heat. During the operation, the physician had to stop drilling every

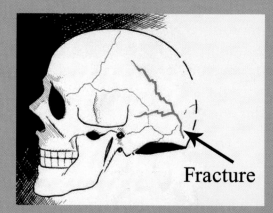

Fracture

A skull with a fracture

so often to dip the drill into cold water. If he didn't, he would burn away the bone around hole. The constant starts and stops dragged out the procedure. Patients had to endure the pain that much longer.

Chronology

460 BCE	Is born on the Greek island of Cos
*	Completes medical studies, leaves Cos
*	Cures plague in Athens
*	Treats illness of Perdiccas, king of Macedonia
*	Travels to Abdera to treat Democritus
*	Turns down request to travel to Persian Empire to treat plague
*	Records details of his procedures and case studies
377 BCE	Dies in Larissa, Thessaly

* Events that may have happened, but there is no way of knowing when they occurred

BIOGRAPHY FROM
ANCIENT CIVILIZATIONS
LEGENDS, FOLKLORE, AND STORIES OF ANCIENT WORLDS

Timeline in History

BCE

c. 1200 Legendary date of the Trojan War.

c. 800 Homer writes *The Iliad*, which includes details of medical treatment available for wounded soldiers.

c. 600 Greek thinkers began seeking scientific explanations for natural phenomena.

507 Athens forms the world's first democratic government.

480 The threat of a Persian invasion ends with Greek victory at the Battle of Salamis, which leads to a flowering of Greek ideas.

469 Athenian philosopher Socrates is born.

431 The Peloponnesian War, which divides Greece into two warring factions, begins.

430 Plague breaks out in Athens.

404 Sparta defeats Athens to end the Peloponnesian War.

399 Socrates is executed.

384 Greek philosopher Aristotle is born; he becomes interested in studying natural events.

336 Alexander the Great becomes king of Macedonia and begins a program of conquest.

332 Alexander founds the city of Alexandria, which becomes the center of Greek learning and remains so for several centuries.

323 Alexander the Great dies.

322 Aristotle dies.

146 Greece falls under Roman control.

CE

129 The noted Roman physician Galen is born.

199 Galen dies.

476 The Western Roman Empire falls and scholars (including physicians) soon lose contact with Greek thinking.

622 Muhammad's journey to Medina marks the beginning of the religion of Islam; Islamic scholars preserve the writings of Hippocrates and other ancient Greeks.

c. 1200 Greek writings begin filtering back to the West.

1453 Constantinople, the center of learning of the Eastern Roman Empire, falls; many scholars flee to the West and dramatically increase knowledge about ancient Greeks.

c. 1500 Western physicians begin questioning information in Greek medical texts, but use Greek methods of observation and practice to develop modern medicine.

Chapter Notes

Chapter 1
Time-Tested Medical Treatments
 1. "Bee Therapy Popular in China," *People's Daily,* May 14, 2001, http://english.people.com.cn/english/200105/14/eng20010514_69867.html
Chapter 2
Early Greek Medicine
 1. Peter James and Nick Thorpe, *Ancient Inventions* (New York: Ballantine Books, 1994), p. 2.
 2. Homer, *The Iliad*, translated by Robert Fagles (New York: Penguin Books, 1990), p. 324.
 3. Ibid.
 4. Guido Majno, *The Healing Hand: Man and Wound in the Ancient World* (Cambridge, Massachusetts: Harvard University Press, 1975), p. 201.
 5. Ibid., p. 205.
Chapter 3
A Legendary Life
 1. David Noy, *Ancient Medicine: Myth and Practice,* "Hippocrates," http://www.lamp.ac.uk/~noy/Medicine1.htm
 2. Edwin Burton Levine, *Hippocrates* (New York: Twayne Publishers, 1971), p. 15.
 3. Thucydides, *History of the Peloponnesian War,* translated by Rex Warner (New York: Penguin, 1954), pp. 152–155.

 4. Ann Ellis Hanson, *Hippocrates: The "Greek Miracle" in Medicine,* http://www.medicinaantiqua.org.uk/sa_hippint.html
Chapter 4
The Hippocratic Collection
 1. David Noy, *Ancient Medicine: Myth and Practice,* "Hippocrates," http://www.lamp.ac.uk/~noy/Medicine1.htm
 2. William F. Petersen, M.D., *Hippocratic Wisdom* (Springfield, Illinois: Charles C. Thomas, 1946), pp. 41–42.
 3. Ann Ellis Hanson, *Hippocrates: The "Greek Miracle" in Medicine,* http://www.medicinaantiqua.org.uk/sa_hippint.html
 4. Petersen, p. 40.
 5. Ibid., pp. 66–67.
 6. Ibid., pp. 82–83.
 7. Ibid., p. 56.
 8. Edwin Burton Levine, *Hippocrates* (New York: Twayne Publishers, 1971), p. 82.
 9. Ibid.
 10. Peter James and Nick Thorpe. *Ancient Inventions* (New York: Ballantine Books, 1994), p. 5.
 11. Levine, pp. 57–58.
Chapter 5
After Hippocrates
 1. Roy Porter, *Blood and Guts: A Short History of Medicine* (New York: W. W. Norton, 2003), p. 34.

Further Reading

For Young Adults

Nardo, Don. *Greek and Roman Science.* San Diego, California: Lucent Books, 1998.

Parker, Steve. *Medicine.* New York: DK Publishing, 2000.

Pearson, Anne. *Ancient Greece.* New York: DK Publishing, 2004.

Woods, Michael, and Mary B. Woods. *Ancient Medicine: From Sorcery to Surgery.* Minneapolis: Runestone Press, 2000.

Works Consulted

Cantor, David (editor). *Reinventing Hippocrates.* Burlington, Vermont: Ashgate Publishing Company, 2002.

Haggard, Howard W. *The Doctor in History.* New York: Dorset Press, 1989.

Homer. *The Iliad.* Translated by Robert Fagles. New York: Penguin Books, 1990.

James, Peter, and Nick Thorpe. *Ancient Inventions.* New York: Ballantine Books, 1994.

Levine, Edwin Burton. *Hippocrates.* New York: Twayne Publishers, 1971.

Majno, Guido. *The Healing Hand: Man and Wound in the Ancient World.* Cambridge, Massachusetts: Harvard University Press, 1975.

Petersen, William F., M.D. *Hippocratic Wisdom.* Springfield, Illinois: Charles C. Thomas, 1946.

Plutarch. *Plutarch's Lives: Volume II.* Translated by John Dryden. Revised and edited by Arthur Hugh Clough. New York: Modern Library, 1992.

Porter, Roy. *Blood and Guts: A Short History of Medicine.* New York: W. W. Norton, 2003.

Porter, Roy (editor). *Medicine: A History of Healing.* Lewes, United Kingdom: The Ivy Press, 1997.

Root-Bernstein, Robert, and Michèle Root-Bernstein. *Honey, Mud, Maggots, and Other Medical Marvels: The Science Behind Folk Remedies and Old Wives' Tales.* New York: Houghton Mifflin, 1997.

On the Internet

Antiqua Medicina: From Homer to Vesalius http://www.med.virginia.edu/hs-library/historical/antiqua/textf.htm

"Bee Therapy Popular in China." *People's Daily.* May 14, 2001. http://english.people.com.cn/english/200105/14/eng20010514_69867.html

Chavez, Paul. "Korean War Vet to Get Medal of Honor After 55 Years." Associated Press. September 17, 2005. http://aolsvc.news.aol.com/news/article.adp?id=20050917061509990001

Mauthausen Concentration Camp (Austria) http://www.jewishgen.org/ForgottenCamps/Camps/MauthausenEng.html

Noy, David. *Ancient Medicine: Myth and Practice.* "Hippocrates." http://www.lamp.ac.uk/~noy/Medicine1.htm

Than, Ker. "Maggots and Leeches: Old Medicine Is New." *Live Science.* April 19, 2005. http://www.livescience.com/humanbiology/050419_maggots.html

Glossary

archaeologists — (ar-kee-AH-luh-jists)—scientists who study the lives and habits of people who lived in ancient civilizations.

consecrated — (KON-suh-kray-ted)—made sacred.

excrement — (EK-skruh-munt)—solid bodily waste.

fecal matter — (FEE-kul MAA-tur)—solid bodily waste.

larvae — (LAR-vee)—immature, often wormlike insect hatchlings.

latrines — (luh-TREENZ)—earthen pits used to hold human waste.

quarry — (KWAH-ree)—an open mine that contains masses of useful stone such as marble or granite.

salves — (SAVZ)—soothing substances applied to wounds or sores to ease pain and help with the healing process.

scleroderma — (skler-uh-DER-muh)—a disease characterized by a thickening of the skin.

supernatural — (soo-per-NAA-chuh-rul)—coming from a god or some other invisible or unobservable source.

suppurated — (SUH-pyuh-ray-ted)—filled with or discharging pus.

ulcer — (UL-sur)—an open sore that occurs on the skin or in the stomach lining.

Index